Newport Community Learning
and Libraries

Z685682

KU-303-156

The Land of Counterpane
and other poems

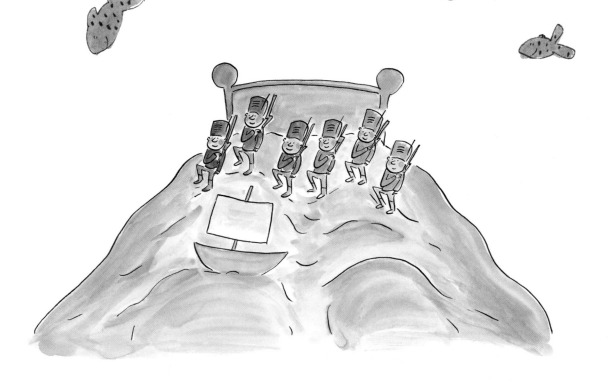

Compiled by Tig Thomas

Miles Kelly

First published in 2010 by Miles Kelly Publishing Ltd
Harding's Barn, Bardfield End Green, Thaxted, Essex, CM6 3PX, UK

Copyright © Miles Kelly Publishing Ltd 2010

2 4 6 8 10 9 7 5 3 1

Editorial Director Belinda Gallagher

Art Director Jo Cowan

Assistant Editor Claire Philip

Designer Joe Jones

Junior Designer Kayleigh Allen

Production Manager Elizabeth Collins

Reprographics Stephan Davis, Ian Paulyn

All rights reserved. No part of this publication may be reproduced, stored in a
retrieval system, or transmitted by any means, electronic, mechanical, photocopying,
recording or otherwise, without the prior permission of the copyright holder.

ISBN 978-1-84810-367-2

Printed in China

British Library Cataloguing-in-Publication Data
A catalogue record for this book is available from the British Library

ACKNOWLEDGEMENTS

The publishers would like to thank Kirsten Wilson for
the illustrations she contributed to this book.

All other artwork from the Miles Kelly Artwork Bank

The publishers would like to thank Elena Kalistratova/iStockphoto.com
for the use of their photograph on page 4.

Made with paper from a sustainable forest

www.mileskelly.net
info@mileskelly.net

www.factsforprojects.com

Self-publish your
children's book

buddingpress.co.uk

Contents

From # The Masque of Oberon

Buzz! Quoth the Blue-fly
Hum! Quoth the Bee
Buzz and hum! They cry
And so do we
In his ear! In his nose!
Thus, – do you see?
He ate the dormouse –
Else it was he.

Ben Jonson

Hum hum hum!

Masque an old type of play often set to music with masked actors

Buzz buzz buzz!

From Robin Hood

Yet let us sing
Honour to the old bow-string!
Honour to the bugle-horn!
Honour to the woods unshorn!
Honour to the Lincoln green!
Honour to the archer keen!

Honour to tight little John,
And the horse he rode upon!
Honour to bold Robin Hood,
Sleeping in the underwood!
Honour to maid Marian,
And to all the Sherwood clan!

John Keats

Mr Nobody

I know a funny little man,
As quiet as a mouse,
Who does the mischief that is done
In everybody's house!
There's no one ever sees his face,
And yet we all agree
That every plate we break was cracked
By Mr Nobody.

'Tis he who always tears our books,
Who leaves the door ajar,
Who pulls the buttons from our shirts,
And scatters pins afar;
That squeaking door will always squeak
For, prithee, don't you see,
We leave the oiling to be done
By Mr Nobody.

He puts damp wood upon the fire,
That kettles cannot boil;
His are the feet that bring in mud,
And all the carpets soil.
The papers always are mislaid,
Who had them last but he?
There's no one tosses them about
But Mr Nobody.

The finger marks upon the door
By none of us are made;
We never leave the blinds unclosed,
To let the curtains fade.
The ink we never spill, the boots
That lying round you see,
Are not our boots; they all belong
To Mr Nobody.

Anonymous

From The Mermaid

Who would be
A mermaid fair,
Singing alone,
Combing her hair
Under the sea,
In a golden curl
With a comb of
    pearl,
On a throne?

I would be a
    mermaid fair;
I would sing to myself the
    whole of the day;
With a comb of pearl I
    would comb my hair;
And still as I comb'd I
    would sing and say,
Who is it loves me? who loves not me?
I would comb my hair till my ringlets would fall
Low adown, low adown,

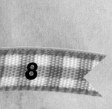

From under my starry sea-bud crown
Low adown and around,
And I should look like a fountain of gold
Springing alone
With a shrill inner sound,
Over the throne
In the midst of the hall;
Till that great sea snake under the sea
From his coiled sleeps in the central deeps
Would slowly trail himself sevenfold
Round the hall where I sate, and look in at the gate
With his large calm eyes for the love of me.
And all the mermen under the sea
  Would feel their immortality
    Die in their hearts for the love of me.

Alfred, Lord Tennyson

The Merman

Who would be
A merman bold,
Sitting alone,
Singing alone
Under the sea,
With a crown of gold,
On a throne?

I would be a merman bold,
I would sit and sing the whole of the day;
I would fill the sea-halls with a voice of power;
    But at night I would roam abroad and play
    With the mermaids in and out of the rocks,
    Dressing their hair with the white sea-flower;

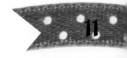

And holding them back by their flowing locks
I would kiss them often under the sea,
And kiss them again till they kiss'd me
Laughingly, laughingly;
And then we would wander away, away
To the pale-green sea-groves straight and high,
Chasing each other merrily.

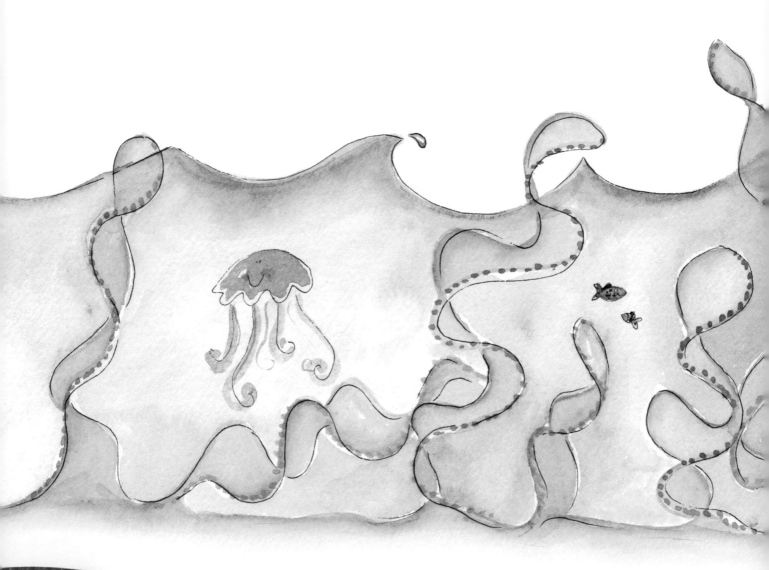

There would be neither moon nor star;
But the wave would make music above us afar –
Low thunder and light in the magic night –
Neither moon nor star…

Oh! What a happy life were mine
Under the hollow-hung ocean green!
Soft are the moss-beds under the sea;
We would live merrily, merrily.

Alfred, Lord Tennyson

From *An Angel's Visit*

Tonight we heard a call,
A rattle on the windowpane,
A voice on the sharp air,
And felt a breath stirring our hair,
A flame within us — something swift and tall
Swept in and out and that was all.

Was it a bright or a dark angel? Who can know?
It left no mark upon the snow,
But suddenly it snapped the chain
Unbarred, flung wide the door.
Which will not shut again;
And so we cannot sit here any more.

We must rise and go:

The world is cold without

And dark and hedged about

With mystery and eternity and doubt,

But we must go

Although yet we do not know

Who called, or what marks we shall
    leave upon the snow.

Charlotte Mew

From The Butterfly's Ball and the Grasshopper's Feast

Come take up your Hats, and away let us haste
To the Butterfly's Ball, and the Grasshopper's Feast.
The Trumpeter, Gadfly, has summon'd the Crew,
And the Revels are now only waiting for you.

And there was the Gnat and the Dragonfly too,
With all their Relations, Green, Orange, and Blue.
And there came the Moth, with his Plumage of Down,
And the Hornet in Jacket of Yellow and Brown;

Who with him the Wasp, his Companion, did bring,
But they promis'd, that Evening, to lay by their Sting.
And the sly little Dormouse crept out of his Hole,
And brought to the Feast his blind Brother, the Mole.

And the Snail, with his Horns peeping out of his Shell,
Came from a great Distance, the Length of an Ell.
A Mushroom their Table, and on it was laid
Water-dock Leaf, which a Tablecloth made.

William Roscoe

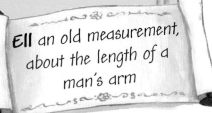

Ell an old measurement, about the length of a man's arm

My Fairy

I have a fairy by my side
Which says I must not sleep,
When once in pain I loudly cried
It said "**You must not weep.**"

If, full of mirth, I smile and grin,
It says "**You must not laugh;**"
When once I wished to drink some gin
It said "**You must not quaff.**"

When once a meal I wished to taste
It said "**You must not bite,**"
When to the wars I went in haste
It said "**You must not fight.**"

"**What may I do?**" at length I cried,
Tired of the painful task.
The fairy quietly replied,
And said "**You must not ask.**"

Moral: "**You mustn't**"

Lewis Carroll

From *Fairy Feast*

Upon a mushroom's head
Our tablecloth we spread;
A grain of rye, or wheat,
Is manchet, which we eat;
Pearly drops of dew we drink
In acorn cups fill'd to the brink.

The brains of nightingales,
With unctuous fat of snails,
Between two cockles stew'd,
Is meat that's easily chew'd;
Tails of worms, and marrow of mice,
Do make a dish that's wondrous nice.

Anonymous

Manchet a loaf of fine white bread
Unctuous oily

From The Noon Call

Sprightly, lightly,
Sing we rightly!
Moments brightly hurry away!
Fruit-tree blossoms,
And roses' bosoms
Clear blue sky of a summer day!
Dear blue sky of a summer day!

Springlets, brooklets,
Greeny nooklets,
Hill and valley, and salt-sea spray!
Comrade rovers,
Fairy lovers,
All the length of a summer day!
All the livelong summer day!

William Allingham

From *Two Fairies in a Garden*

O, far away,

Over river must we fly,

Over the sea and the mountain high,

Over city, seen afar

Like a low and misty star,

Soon beneath us glittering

Like million spark-worms. But our wing,

For the flight will ne'er suffice.

Some are training Flittermice,

I a Silver Moth."

William Allingham

Flittermice bats
Suffice be enough

The Fairy Pigwiggin Arms for the Fight

A little cockle-shell his shield,
Which he could very bravely wield,

Yet could it not be pierced –
His spear a bent both stiff and strong
And well-near of two inches long,
The pile was of a housefly's tongue
Whose sharpness naught reversed.

And puts him on a coat of mail,
Which was of a fish's scale,
That when his foe should him assail

No point should be prevailing:
His rapier was a hornet's sting,
It was a very dangerous thing;
For if he chanced to hurt the King
It would be long in healing.

Bent a stiff grass-stalk
Mettle courage
Pile the pointed metal head of spear
Rapier sharply pointed sword

His helmet was a beetle's head,
Most horrible and full of dread,
That able was to strike one dead,

Yet did it well become him;
And for a plume a horse's hair,
Which, being tossed with the air,
Had force to strike his foe with fear

And turn his weapon from him.
Himself he on an earwig set,
Yet scarce he on his back could get,
So oft and high he did curvet
Ere he himself could settle:

He made him turn and stop and bound,
To gallop and to trot the round;
He scarce could stand on any ground,
He was so full of mettle.

Michael Drayton

The Elves' Goodbye

The moonlight fades from flower and tree,
And the stars dim one by one;
The tale is told, the song is sung,
And the Fairy feast is done.
The night-wind rocks the sleeping flowers,
And sings to them, soft and low.
The early birds erelong will wake –
'Tis time for the Elves to go.

O'er the sleeping earth we silently pass,
Unseen by mortal eye,
And send sweet dreams, as we lightly float
Through the quiet moonlit sky;
For the stars' soft eyes alone may see,
And the flowers alone may know,
The feasts we hold, the tales we tell –
So 'tis time for the Elves to go.

From bird, and blossom, and bee,
We learn the lessons they teach;
And seek, by kindly deeds, to win
A loving friend in each.
And though unseen on earth we dwell,
Sweet voices whisper low,
And gentle hearts most joyously greet
The Elves where'er they go.

When next we meet in the Fairy dell,
May the silver moon's soft light
Shine then on faces gay as now,
And Elfin hearts as light.
Now spread each wing, for the eastern sky
With sunlight soon will glow.
The morning star shall light us home –
Farewell! For the Elves must go.

Louisa M Alcott

Me and my Brother

In form and feature, face and limb,
I grew so like my brother,
That folks got taking me for him,
And each for one another.

It puzzled all our kith and kin,
It reached a fearful pitch;
For one of us was born a twin,
Yet not a soul knew which.

One day, to make the matter worse,
Before our names were fixed,
As we were being washed by nurse,
We got completely mixed;

And thus, you see, by fate's decree,
Or rather nurse's whim,
My brother John got christened me,
And I got christened him.

This fatal likeness even dogged
My footsteps when at school,
And I was always getting flogged,
For John turned out a fool.

I put this question, fruitlessly,
To everyone I knew,
"What would you do, if you were me,
To prove that you were you?"

Our close resemblance turned the tide
Of my domestic life,
For somehow, my intended bride
Became my brother's wife.

In fact, year after year the same
Absurd mistakes went on,
And when I died, the neighbours came
And buried brother John.

Henry S Leigh

The Last Voyage of the Fairies

Down the bright stream the Fairies float,
A water lily is their boat.

Long rushes they for paddles take,
Their mainsail of a bat's wing make;

The tackle is of cobwebs neat,
With glowworm lantern all's complete.

So down the broad'ning stream they float,
With Puck as pilot of the boat.

The Queen on speckled moth-wings lies,
And lifts at times her languid eyes

To mark the green and mossy spots
Where bloom the blue forget-me-nots –

Oberon, on his rosebud throne,
Claims the fair valley as his own –

And elves and fairies, with a shout
Which may be heard a yard about,

Hail him as Elfland's mighty King;
And hazelnuts in homage bring,

And bend the unreluctant knee,
And wave their wands in loyalty.

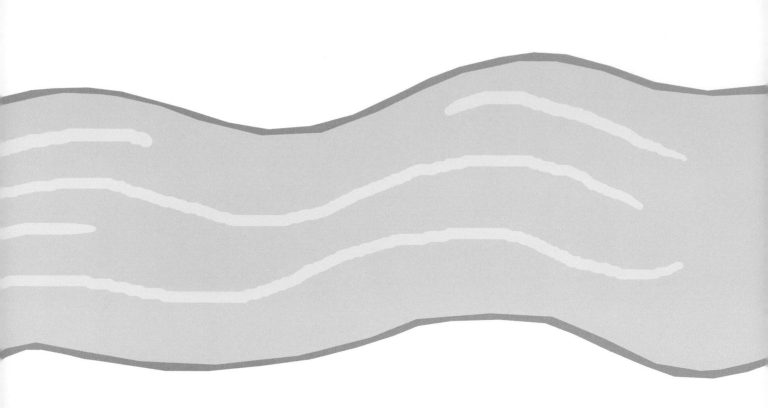

Down the broad stream the Fairies float,
An unseen power impels their boat;

The banks fly past – each wooded scene –
The elder copse – the poplars green –

And soon they feel the briny breeze
With salt and savour of the seas –

Still down the stream the Fairies float,
An unseen power impels their boat;

Until they mark the rushing tide
Within the estuary wide.

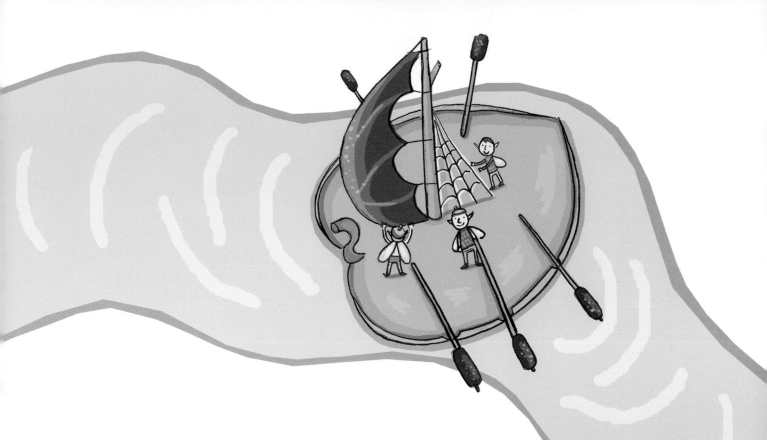

And now they're tossing on the sea,
Where waves roll high, and winds blow free,

Ah, mortal vision nevermore
Shall see the Fairies on the shore,

Or watch upon a summer night
Their mazy dances of delight!

Far, far away upon the sea,
The waves roll high, the breeze blows free!

The Queen on speckled moth-wings lies,
Slow gazing with a strange surprise

Where swim the sea-nymphs on the tide
Or on the backs of dolphins ride –

The King, upon his rosebud throne,
Pales as he hears the waters moan;

The elves have ceased their sportive play,
Hushed by the slowly sinking day –

And still afar, afar they float,
The Fairies in their fragile boat,

Further and further from the shore,
And lost to mortals evermore!

W H Davenport Adams

Jerry Hall

Jerry Hall, he was so small,
A rat could eat him, hat and all.

Anonymous

The Land of Counterpane

When I was sick and lay a-bed,
I had two pillows at my head,
And all my toys beside me lay
To keep me happy all the day.

And sometimes for an hour or so
I watched my leaden soldiers go,
With different uniforms and drills,
Among the bed clothes,
    through the hills;

And sometimes sent my ships in fleets
All up and down among the sheets;
Or brought my trees and houses out,
And planted cities all about.

I was the giant great and still
That sits upon the pillow-hill,
And sees before him, dale and plain,
The pleasant land of counterpane.

Robert Louis Stevenson

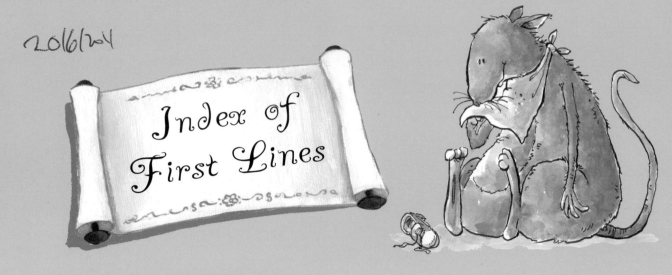

Index of First Lines

Newport Community Learning & Libraries	
Z685682	
PETERS	07-Apr-2011
J821.008	£5.99